St. Paul's Anglican Churchyard A-B

The Grave Whisperer

Angeline Gallant

Published by Angeline Gallant, 2022.

While every precaution has been taken in the preparation of this book, the publisher assumes no responsibility for errors or omissions, or for damages resulting from the use of the information contained herein.

ST. PAUL'S ANGLICAN CHURCHYARD A-B

First edition. September 4, 2022.

Written by Angeline Gallant.

Also by Angeline Gallant

A Dragon's Diary
Dreaming of Dragons

Blood and Spirit Saga
The Rising Wind

Calling Her Heart
Whisper of the Heart
Calling Her Heart Volumes 1 & 2: A Small Town Romance Collection
No Turning Back
Calling Her Heart volumes 3 & 4
Forsake Me Not
Hear My Cry

FORGET ME NOT
Victoria, Ontario's Babies 1894 - 1895

GENERATIONS OF THE VOLGA
A Family's Legacy

Guardian of the Heart
Fallen Petals

Keeper Of Secrets
A Lady's Secret

Kingston's Love Chronicles
Springtime Promises

Midnight's Awakening
Heart of the Storm
Walking Through The Storm
Walking Through The Storm
Fighting the Storm
Call Me Cursed
Heart of the Storm

Secrets of the Underworld
Deklan's Dragons

Cataraqui United Church Cemetery 6
Beneath the Surface: Echoes from Beth Israel Cemetery
Grave Tales: Discovering the Lives of Beth Israel

The Timeless Veil
Eternal Devotion

The Wolf Whisperer Series
Captured Heart
Fate's Legacy
Mohawk Valley
Cry of a Warrior
Wolf Whisperer volumes 1 & 2
Endless White
The Wolf Whisperer volumes 1 & 2

Timeless
The Time Keeper's Sanctuary

Timeless Whispers of Dervock Saga
Secrets of Dervock

Standalone
Winds of Change vol 1-3

Table of Contents

ELIZABETH ADAMS[1]

Elizabeth passed away in February 1814 and was buried in Kingston, Frontenac, Upper Canada, British Colonial America. A church was built over her grave.

ELIZABETH "ELIZA" (JENKINS) ADAMS[2]

Eliza was born on June 20, 1765 in England. She was 27 years old when she married Captain James Adams on October 28, 1792 in Richmond, England.

Eliza was 28 years old when her daughter, Sara, was born in Edwardsburgh, Ontario in 1793.

She was 29 years old when her son, William, was born in Kingston in 1794.

Eliza was 35 years old when her daughter, Elizabeth Betsy, was born in Edwardsburgh in 1800.

She was 37 years old when her son, James, passed away on August 14, 1802 in Kingston. Her daughter, Sara, passed away a few days later on August 23rd.

Eliza was around 38 years old when her daughter, Mary Ann was born.

She was 40 years old when her son, Henry, was born in Kingston in 1806.

Eliza was 43 years old when her daughter, Eleanor, was born in Kingston in 1808.

She was 46 years old when the War of 1812 took place.

Eliza was 48 years old when she passed away on December 21, 1813. She was buried in Kingston, Frontenac, Upper Canada, British Colonial America. A church was built over her grave.

CPT. JAMES ADAMS[3]

James was born in 1765.

He was 26 years old when the first parliament of Upper Canada assembled on September 17, 1791.

James was 54 years old when he passed away in 1819. He was buried in Kingston, Frontenac, Upper Canada, British Colonial America. A church was built over his grave.

JAMES ADAMS[4]

James was buried on August 14, 1802 in Kingston, Frontenac, Upper Canada, British Colonial America. A church was built over his grave.

SARA ADAMS[5]

Sara was born on September 24, 1793 in Edwardsburgh, Ontario. She was a year old when her brother, William, was born in Kingston in 1794.

Sara was six years old when her sister, Elizabeth Betsy, was born in Edwardsburgh in 1800.

She was eight years old when her brother, James, was buried on August 14th, 1802. Sarah passed away a few days later and was buried on August 23rd in Kingston, Frontenac, Upper Canada, British Colonial America. A church was built over her grave.

DANIEL ALLIN ADKINS[6]

Daniel passed away in 1826 and was buried in Kingston, Frontenac, Upper Canada, British Colonial America. A church was built over his grave.

WILLIAM AIKIN[7]

William was buried on September 13, 1802 in Kingston, Frontenac, Upper Canada, British Colonial America. A church was built over his grave.

ALEXANDER AITKEN[8]

Alexander was a surveyor.

He passed away in 1799 and was buried in Kingston, Frontenac, Upper Canada, British Colonial America. A church was built over his grave.

WILLIAM ANDERSON[9]

William was buried on January 11, 1805 in Kingston, Frontenac, Upper Canada, British Colonial America. A church was built over his grave.

ANN ARKLAND[10]

Ann was buried on May 14, 1809 in Kingston, Frontenac, Upper Canada, British Colonial America. A church was built over her grave.

JOSEPH ASHLEY[11]

J oseph was born on August 25, 1801 in Kingston, Frontenac, Upper
Canada, British Colonial America.

He was buried on August 20, 1802 in Kingston, five days before his first
birthday. A church was built over his grave.

CPL. THOMAS ASKEY[12]

T homas was buried on June 29, 1794 in Kingston, Frontenac, Upper Canada, British Colonial America. A church was built over his grave.

MARY ASKEY[13]

———

Mary was buried on October 3, 1801 in Kingston, Frontenac, Upper Canada, British Colonial America. A church was built over her grave.

JANE ATKINSON[14]

Jane was buried on October 5, 1819 in Kingston, Frontenac, Upper Canada, British Colonial America. A church was built over her grave.

MARY ATKINSON[15]

Mary passed away in 1827 and was buried in Kingston, Frontenac, Upper Canada, British Colonial America. A church was built over her grave.

WILLIAM ATKINSON[16]

William passed away in 1825 and was buried in Kingston, Frontenac, Upper Canada, British Colonial America. A church was built over his grave.

WILLIAM ATKINSON ESQ.[17]

William was buried on April 10, 1805 in Kingston, Frontenac, Upper Canada, British Colonial America. A church was built over his grave.

WILLIAM ATKINSON[18]

William passed away in 1813 and was buried in Kingston, Frontenac, Upper Canada, British Colonial America. A church was built over his grave.

ROBERT WALKER ATKISON[19]

Robert passed away in 1812 and was buried in Kingston, Frontenac, Upper Canada, British Colonial America. A church was built over his grave.

JOHN AUSTIN[20]

John passed away in 1816 and was buried in Kingston, Frontenac, Upper Canada, British Colonial America. A church was built over his grave.

REBEKAH AUSTIN[21]

Rebekah passed away in 1815 and is buried in Kingston, Frontenac, Upper Canada, British Colonial America. A church was built over her grave.

W. AYKROUD[22]

It is believed that he was an infant when he passed away in 1812. He was buried in Kingston, Frontenac, Upper Canada, British Colonial America and a church was built over his grave.

SARAH BADGLEY[23]

Sarah was buried on May 6, 1841 in Kingston, Frontenac, Upper Canada, British Colonial America. A church was built over her grave.

WILLIAM BADGLEY[24]

William was buried on March 20, 1798 in Kingston, Frontenac, Upper Canada, British Colonial America. A church was built over his grave.

WILLIAM BAIN[25]

William passed away in 1823 and was buried in Kingston, Frontenac, Upper Canada, British Colonial America. A church was built over his grave.

CHARLES BAKER JR. [26]

25

Charles passed away in 1823 and was buried in Kingston, Frontenac, Upper Canada, British Colonial America. A church was built over his grave.

HANNAH MARIA BAKER[27]

Hannah passed away in 1815 and was buried in Kingston, Frontenac, Upper Canada, British Colonial America. A church was built over her grave.

CPT. JAMES BAKER E.U.L.[28]

James was buried on April 11, 1800 in Kingston, Frontenac, Upper Canada, British Colonial America. A church was built over his grave.

MATTHEW BALFOUR[29]

Matthew was born on August 18, 1818 in Kingston, Frontenac, Upper Canada, British Colonial America.

He passed away a month later on September 30, 1818 and is buried in Kingston. A church was built over his grave.

JULIA BALLAN[30]

Julia was buried on November 11, 1796 in Kingston, Frontenac, Upper Canada, British Colonial America. A church was built over her grave.

CHARLES BAMFORD[31]

Charles passed away in 1826 and was buried in Kingston, Frontenac, Upper Canada, British Colonial America. A church was built over his grave.

JOHN BARNES[32]

John was buried on October 21, 1803 in Kingston, Frontenac, Upper Canada, British Colonial America. A church was built over his grave.

JANE BARNS[33]

Jane was buried on April 23, 1803 in Kingston, Frontenac, Upper Canada, British Colonial America. A church was built over her grave.

JOSIAH BARRICE[34]

Josiah was buried on October 24, 1795 in Kingston, Frontenac, Upper Canada, British Colonial America. A church was built over his grave.

NANCY (RUSSELL) BARTLET[35]

Nancy was born on July 7, 1782 in Providence, Rhode Island. She was 12 years old when her brother, Capt. John Newton Russell, passed away on September 11, 1794.

Nancy was 16 years old when her sister, Mehitable, passed away on November 6, 1798. Her mother passed away a month later on December 16th.

She was 17 years old when her sister, Martha, passed away on April 7, 1800.

Nancy was 20 years old when she married Smith on September 26, 1802 in Cumberland, Rhode Island.

She was 29 years old when the War of 1812 took place.

Nancy was 31 when her father passed away in 1813.

She was 34 years old when her sister, Amy Mary, passed away in 1817.

Nancy was 36 years old when she passed away on November 11, 1819 in Kingston, Frontenac, Upper Canada, British Colonial America where she is buried.

JOHN BATEMAN[36]

John was buried on April 28, 1811 in Kingston, Frontenac, Upper Canada, British Colonial America. A church was built over his grave.

UNKNOWN BAYMANS[37]

James Baymans' child was buried on May 13, 1810 in Kingston, Frontenac, Upper Canada, British Colonial America. A church was built over the grave.

JAMES BAYMAN[38]

J ames was buried on November 17, 1799 in Kingston, Frontenac, Upper Canada, British Colonial America. A church was built over his grave.

ADAM BEARD[39]

Adam was buried on October 15, 1805 in Kingston, Frontenac, Upper Canada, British Colonial America. A Church was built over his grave.

CAPT. ANTOINE MARTIN BEAUBIEN[40]

A ntoine was born on October 17, 1756 in Quebec, Canada, New France.

He was 34 years old when the first parliament of Upper Canada assembled on September 17, 1791.

Antoine was buried on April 18, 1800 in Kingston, Frontenac, Upper Canada, British Colonial America. He was 43 years old. A church was built over his grave.

WILLIAM BEEMAN[41]

William was buried on June 5, 1799 in Kingston, Frontenac, Upper Canada, British Colonial America. A church was built over his grave.

JOHN BELFLEUR[42]

John was buried on February 26, 1805 in Kingston, Frontenac, Upper Canada, British Colonial America. A church was built over his grave.

ROBERT BETSON[43]

R obert was buried on October 28, 1805 in Kingston, Frontenac, Upper Canada, British Colonial America. A church was built over his grave.

COMO DAVID BETTON[44]

Como passed away on October 11, 1794. He was buried on October 17th in Kingston, Frontenac, Upper Canada, British Colonial America. A church was built over his grave.

ANN BLACKWOOD[45]

Ann was buried on May 3, 1805 in Kingston, Frontenac, Upper Canada, British Colonial America. A church was built over her grave.

GEORGE BLAIN[46]

George was buried on May 22, 1810 in Kingston, Frontenac, Upper Canada, British Colonial America. A church was built over his grave. He was a sailor.

GEORGE BLOOM[47]

George passed away in 1813 and was buried in Kingston, Frontenac, Upper Canada, British Colonial America. A church was built over his grave.

UNKNOWN BOINTON[48]

—

She was only a child when she was buried on August 10, 1804 in Kingston, Frontenac, Upper Canada, British Colonial America. A church was built over her grave.

EUGENIA BOINTON[49]

Eugenia was buried on August 31, 1804 in Kingston, Frontenac, Upper Canada, British Colonial America. A church was built over her grave.

CATHERINE ANNE BONNYCASTLE[50]

Catherine was born on December 18, 1829 in Kingston, Frontenac, Upper Canada, British Colonial America.

She was three years old when the Factory Act was passed in 1833. Her baby sister, Georgiana, passed away the same year on August 25th.

Catherine was 13 years old when "A Christmas Carol" was first published in 1943.

She was 15 years old when she passed away on June 27, 1845 in York, Ontario. Catherine is buried in Kingston, Ontario.

LADY FRANCES (JOHNSTONE) BONNYCASTLE[51]

Frances was born in Scotland in March 1792. She was not yet a year old when the Reign of Terror took place in 1793.

Frances was 20 years old when she married Liet. Col. Sir. Richard Henry Bonnycastle on August 6, 1812 in Edinborough, Scotland.

She was 27 years old when her son, John, passed away in 1819.

Frances was 27 years old when the "Radical War" took place in 1820.

She was 29 years old when her son, Charles, passed away in 1822.

Frances was 32 years old when her son, William Henry John, passed away in 1824.

She was 34 years old when her son, Francis, passed away in 1826.

Frances was 41 years old when her one-year-old daughter, Georgiana, passed away in 1833.

She was 53 years old when her daughter, Catherine Anne, passed away in 1845.

Frances was 55 years old when her husband passed away in 1847.

She was 68 years old when her daughter, Charlotte, passed away in 1860.

Frances was 77 years old when she passed away on July 15, 1869 in Kingston Township, Frontenac, Ontario where she is buried.

LIEUT. COL. SIR. RICHARD HENRY BONNYCASTLE[52]

Richard was born on September 30, 1791 in Woolwich, England. He was six years old when the Young Ireland rebellion failed in 1798.

Richard was 20 years old when he married Lady Frances Johnstone on August 6, 1812 in Edinborough, Scotland.

He was 23 years old when Napoleon Boneparte was defeated in 1815.

Richard was 27 years old when his son, John, passed away in 1819.

He was 29 years old when his father passed away in 1821.

Richard was 30 when his son, Charles, passed away in 1822.

He was 31 years old when rugby football was invented in 1823.

Richard was 32 years old when his son, William Henry John, passed away in 1824.

He was 34 years old when his mother passed away in 1825.

Richard was 35 years old when his son, Francis, passed away in 1826.

He was 41 years old when his daughter, Georgiana, passed away in 1833.

Richard was 49 years old when his brother, Charles, passed away in 1840.

He was 53 years old when the Irish Potato Famine took place in 1845. His daughter, Catherine Anne, passed away on June 27th.

Richard was 56 years old when he passed away on November 2, 1847 in Kingston, Frontenac, Canada West, British Colonial America, where he is buried.

ELIZABETH BRAYLEY[53]

Elizabeth was buried on August 8, 1804 in Kingston, Frontenac, Upper Canada, British Colonial America. A church was built over her grave.

WILLIAM BRAYLEY[54]

William passed away in 1812 and was buried in Kingston, Frontenac, Upper Canada, British Colonial America. A church was built over his grave.

GEORGE BRIANT[55]

George passed away in 1821 and was buried in Kingston, Frontenac, Upper Canada, British Colonial America. A church was built over his grave.

SOPHIA BRINDLE[56]

Sophia passed away in 1813 and was buried in Kingston, Frontenac, Upper Canada, British Colonial America. A church was built over her grave.

JOHN CAMP BROOKS[57]

John was buried on November 7, 1809 in Kingston, Frontenac, Upper Canada, British Colonial America. A church was built over his grave.

MARY BROWN[58]

Mary was buried with Richard Brown on November 26, 1795 in Kingston, Frontenac, Upper Canada, British Colonial America. A church was built over her grave.

RICHARD BROWN[59]

R ichard was buried with Mary Brown on November 26, 1795 in Kingston, Frontenac, Upper Canada, British Colonial America. A church was built over his grave.

MRS. BUCHETTE[60]

She was buried with her child on September 6, 1792 in Kingston, Frontenac, Upper Canada, British Colonial America. A church was built over her grave.

UNKNOWN BRUCHETTE[61]

A child who was buried with their mother on September 6, 1792 in Kingston, Frontenac, Upper Canada, British Colonial America. A church was built over the grave.

JOSEPH BURKE[62]

Joseph passed away in 1796 and was buried in Kingston, Frontenac, Upper Canada, British Colonial America. A church was built over his grave.

ROBERT BURLEY[63]

Robert passed away in 1815 and was buried in Kingston, Frontenac, Upper Canada, British Colonial America. A church was built over his grave.

SAMUEL BURLEY[64]

S amuel was buried on August 26, 1802 in Kingston, Frontenac, Upper Canada, British Colonial America. A church was built over his grave.

UNKNOWN BUSH[65]

They were buried on August 14, 1796 in Kingston, Frontenac, Upper Canada, British Colonial America. A church was built over their grave.

JOHN BUTTERWORTH[66]

John was born in 1792.

He was a hatter while living in Kingston.

John was buried on August 21, 1834 in Kingston, Frontenac, Upper Canada, British Colonial America.

[1] https://www.wikitree.com/genealogy/Unknown-Family-Tree-612256

[2] https://www.wikitree.com/genealogy/Jenkins-Family-Tree-12397

[3] https://www.wikitree.com/genealogy/Adams-Family-Tree-31663

[4] https://www.wikitree.com/genealogy/Adams-Family-Tree-29986

[5] https://www.wikitree.com/genealogy/Adams-Family-Tree-31555

[6] https://www.wikitree.com/genealogy/Adkins-Family-Tree-5561

[7] https://www.wikitree.com/genealogy/Aiken-Family-Tree-1225

[8] https://www.wikitree.com/genealogy/Aitken-Family-Tree-1858

[9] https://www.wikitree.com/genealogy/Anderson-Family-Tree-33054

[10] https://www.wikitree.com/genealogy/Arkland-Family-Tree-3

[11] https://www.wikitree.com/genealogy/Ashley-Family-Tree-3128

[12] https://www.wikitree.com/genealogy/Askey-Family-Tree-365

[13] https://www.wikitree.com/genealogy/Askey-Family-Tree-366

[14] https://www.wikitree.com/genealogy/Atkinson-Family-Tree-6420

[15] https://www.wikitree.com/genealogy/Atkinson-Family-Tree-6421

[16] https://www.wikitree.com/genealogy/Atkinson-Family-Tree-7786

[17] https://www.wikitree.com/genealogy/Atkinson-Family-Tree-6422

[18] https://www.wikitree.com/genealogy/Atkinson-Family-Tree-7787

[19] https://www.wikitree.com/genealogy/Atkison-Family-Tree-44

[20] https://www.wikitree.com/genealogy/Austin-Family-Tree-9694

[21] https://www.wikitree.com/genealogy/Austin-Family-Tree-9695

[22] https://www.wikitree.com/genealogy/Aykroud-Family-Tree-1

[23] https://www.wikitree.com/genealogy/Badgley-Family-Tree-241

[24] https://www.wikitree.com/genealogy/Badgley-Family-Tree-242

[25] https://www.wikitree.com/genealogy/Bain-Family-Tree-2447

[26] https://www.wikitree.com/genealogy/Baker-Family-Tree-37449

[27] https://www.wikitree.com/genealogy/Baker-Family-Tree-37450

[28] https://www.wikitree.com/genealogy/Baker-Family-Tree-37451

[29] https://www.wikitree.com/genealogy/Balfour-Family-Tree-1322

[30] https://www.wikitree.com/genealogy/Ballan-Family-Tree-22

[31] https://www.wikitree.com/genealogy/Bamford-Family-Tree-398

[32] https://www.wikitree.com/genealogy/Barnes-Family-Tree-16409

[33] https://www.wikitree.com/genealogy/Barns-Family-Tree-568

[34] https://www.wikitree.com/genealogy/Barrice-Family-Tree-1

[35] https://www.wikitree.com/genealogy/Russell-Family-Tree-20197

[36] https://www.wikitree.com/genealogy/Bateman-Family-Tree-4283

[37] https://www.wikitree.com/genealogy/Baymans-Family-Tree-1

[38] https://www.wikitree.com/genealogy/Bayman-Family-Tree-17

[39] https://www.wikitree.com/genealogy/Beard-Family-Tree-4452

[40] https://www.wikitree.com/genealogy/Beaubien-Family-Tree-327

[41] https://www.wikitree.com/genealogy/Beeman-Family-Tree-752

[42] https://www.wikitree.com/genealogy/Belfleur-Family-Tree-1

[43] https://www.wikitree.com/genealogy/Betson-Family-Tree-37

[44] https://www.wikitree.com/genealogy/Betton-Family-Tree-58

[45] https://www.wikitree.com/genealogy/Blackwood-Family-Tree-755

[46] https://www.wikitree.com/genealogy/Blain-Family-Tree-616

[47] https://www.wikitree.com/genealogy/Bloom-Family-Tree-1738

[48] https://www.wikitree.com/genealogy/Bointon-Family-Tree-13

[49] https://www.wikitree.com/genealogy/Bointon-Family-Tree-12

[50] https://www.wikitree.com/genealogy/Bonnycastle-Family-Tree-4

[51] https://www.wikitree.com/genealogy/Johnstone-Family-Tree-2188

[52] https://www.wikitree.com/genealogy/Bonnycastle-Family-Tree-3

[53] https://www.wikitree.com/genealogy/Brayley-Family-Tree-207

[54] https://www.wikitree.com/genealogy/Brayley-Family-Tree-173

[55] https://www.wikitree.com/genealogy/Briant-Family-Tree-549

[56] https://www.wikitree.com/genealogy/Brindle-Family-Tree-319

[57] https://www.wikitree.com/genealogy/Brooks-Family-Tree-15071

[58] https://www.wikitree.com/genealogy/Brown-Family-Tree-85227

[59] https://www.wikitree.com/genealogy/Brown-Family-Tree-85233

[60] https://www.wikitree.com/genealogy/Buchette-Family-Tree-2

[61] https://www.wikitree.com/genealogy/Buchette-Family-Tree-1

[62] https://www.wikitree.com/genealogy/Burke-Family-Tree-7210

[63] https://www.wikitree.com/genealogy/Burley-Family-Tree-909

[64] https://www.wikitree.com/genealogy/Burley-Family-Tree-910

[65] https://www.wikitree.com/genealogy/Bush-Family-Tree-8948

[66] https://www.wikitree.com/genealogy/Butterworth-Family-Tree-786

Don't miss out!

Visit the website below and you can sign up to receive emails whenever Angeline Gallant publishes a new book. There's no charge and no obligation.

https://books2read.com/r/B-A-QGSI-HGYAC

BOOKS2READ

Connecting independent readers to independent writers.

Did you love *St. Paul's Anglican Churchyard A-B*? Then you should read *St. Paul's Anglican Churchyard C-D*[1] by Angeline Gallant!

[2]

This book records the lives of those who are buried in St. Paul's Anglican Churchyard. It is a stepping stone for further research.

Read more at https://www.goodreads.com/author/show/19703964.Angeline_Gallant.

---

1. https://books2read.com/u/b5KBDR

2. https://books2read.com/u/b5KBDR

Also by Angeline Gallant

GENERATIONS OF THE VOLGA
A Family's Legacy

Guardian of the Heart
Fallen Petals

Keeper Of Secrets
A Lady's Secret

Kingston's Love Chronicles
Springtime Promises

Midnight's Awakening
Heart of the Storm
Walking Through The Storm
Walking Through The Storm
Fighting the Storm
Call Me Cursed
Heart of the Storm

Secrets of the Underworld
Deklan's Dragons

Cataraqui United Church Cemetery 6
Beneath the Surface: Echoes from Beth Israel Cemetery
Grave Tales: Discovering the Lives of Beth Israel

The Timeless Veil
Eternal Devotion

The Wolf Whisperer Series
Captured Heart
Fate's Legacy
Mohawk Valley
Cry of a Warrior
Wolf Whisperer volumes 1 & 2
Endless White
The Wolf Whisperer volumes 1 & 2

Timeless
The Time Keeper's Sanctuary

Timeless Whispers of Dervock Saga
Secrets of Dervock

Standalone
Winds of Change vol 1-3

About the Author

Angeline Gallant traces her roots through generations of Old Stock Canadian heritage, her passion for genealogy as deep and enduring as the forests and fields her ancestors once walked. With a reverence for history and an eye for detail, she weaves stories from the fragments of lives left behind in letters, records, and weathered headstones.

An avid reader and devoted writer, Angeline brings the past to life with a curiosity for heraldry and a deep love for the landscapes that shaped her family's story. Each name and date she uncovers feels less like history and more like coming home, a familiar echo in the vast tapestry of time. For her, these stories are not forgotten—they live, breathing in the quiet spaces of memory and tradition, a testament to lives once lived, now eternal in the pages of her books.

Read more at https://www.goodreads.com/author/show/19703964.Angeline_Gallant.